YOUNG SCIENTISTS INVESTIGATE

Sound and Music

Malcolm Dixon
and Karen Smith

Evans

Evans Brothers Limited

NOTES FOR TEACHERS AND PARENTS

Sounds around you (pages 6-7)
Try to make children more aware of the varieties and sources of sounds around them.

Sound is a vibration (pages 8-9)
Encourage children to use the word "vibration". Let them use rulers and tuning forks to experience vibrations. Tuning forks can be purchased from music stores. The effects of vibrations can also be seen when rice is sprinkled on a drum. When the drum is hit the surface vibrates, causing the rice to jump into the air.

Sounds travel (pages 10-11)
Use the photograph and the apparatus to develop the idea that sound travels, in invisible waves, from its source through the air (and through solids and liquids) to our ears. Remember that sound waves travel in all directions, they are three-dimensional.

Can you hear it? (pages 12-13)
Use the photograph to develop the idea that sound travels away from the source, in this case the triangle, and gets fainter as it does so. If possible let children investigate their ideas at firsthand. When using the radio as a source of sound try to develop the idea of a "fair test", i.e. the volume of the radio should be the same for both parts of the investigation. Discuss the idea that sounds can be heard through the tube because the vibrations are prevented from spreading out. You may need a longer tube than the one in the photograph.

Hearing sounds (pages 14-15)
Remind the children never to insert anything into their ears. The ear drum is easily damaged. When using sharp needles or pins children need to be carefully supervised. An extension activity would be to make a cardboard ear trumpet (cone shaped) and to see if this enabled the children to hear better. Let them observe animals, for example a cat, and discuss how they funnel sounds down their ears.

Making sounds louder (pages 16-17)
Warn children of the possibility of damaging their ears through loud sounds especially when using headphones. Demonstrate increasing the volume (loudness) of a radio. If it is difficult to hear heartbeats through the ribcage, the children should run on the spot for a couple of minutes. Discuss how a doctor uses a stethoscope to listen to sounds in the human body.

Your voice (pages 18-19)
Let the children feel for their voice box. It is more prominent in some individuals than in others. When they say 'aaargh' they may be able to feel the vibrations.

The sound of music (pages 20-21)
Music is made when regular vibrations are made at regular intervals. The instruments referred to here are percussion instruments such as drums, cymbals, triangles, bells, gongs, tambourines and so on. The plant pots can be suspended from the string by using small nails fixed horizontally. The larger pots produce lower notes because they vibrate more slowly.

Blowing musical notes (pages 22-23)
Let children carry out the bottle investigation for themselves. Food colouring can make the water easier to see. Can they make a short tune? Some children may play musical instruments – recorder, flute – which they can demonstrate to others. Use magazines, catalogues and books to collect photographs of wind instruments. When making the wind instrument, moving the cork alters the length of the air column so varying the notes produced when blowing.

Vibrating strings (pages 24-25)
If possible let the children have some first-hand experience of string instruments. Discuss the vibrating strings and the sounds they make. Invite a guitarist or violinist into school to play for the children. Adult help is needed to cut the cardboard on the model guitar. Stretching the bands tighter will make higher sounds. Let the children investigate by using different thicknesses of elastic bands and by varying the lengths of the bands.

Sending sounds (pages 26-27)
When making the telephone use 'hard' string and keep it taut. The sound travels, in the form of vibrations, along the string to the ear. If the string is loose then it cannot vibrate and there is no sound sent.

Bouncing sounds (pages 28-29)
Find a safe place where the children can experience echoes for themselves such as a large empty room, a tunnel, subway or similar construction. Discuss how the sound travels as invisible waves and bounces off the walls back to their ears. When carrying out this experiment you may use the word "reflect" as well as "bounce", i.e. the sound is reflected from the stiff cardboard.

Contents

Sounds around you

There are many kinds of sound and they are made in different ways. Close your eyes. Keep still and listen. What sounds can you hear? Can you hear people talking? Can you hear the sounds of cars? Can you hear children playing? Can you hear any music? What can you hear?

The world is full of different sounds.

Work with a friend

Use a tape-recorder to make a 'sound quiz'. Try to include some of these things on your tape:

You will need:
small tape-recorder

a dog barking
children singing and clapping
water from a tap
music from a radio

a door closing
footsteps
a clock ticking

What other sounds could you include on your tape?

Now see if your friends can guess what the sounds are.

Sound is a vibration

Sounds are made by movements called vibrations. Every sound you hear is made by something vibrating.

In the photograph the girl is flicking the end of a ruler so that it vibrates. She can hear a sound as the end of the ruler moves up and down. Try this simple experiment yourself. Make a long length of ruler vibrate. Make a short length of ruler vibrate. Is there any difference in the sounds? Does the ruler make any sound when it has stopped vibrating?

Feel the vibrations!

Strike a tuning fork gently on a book.
Listen to the sound it makes.
Strike the tuning fork again.
Hold it so that it gently touches your skin.
Can you feel it vibrating?

You will need:
two tuning forks
ping-pong ball
cotton
sticky tape

Fix the cotton to the ping-pong ball with sticky tape.
Strike a tuning fork and hold it next to the hanging ping-pong ball.
What happens? Why does this happen?

Sounds travel

Throw a stone into a pond and you can see small waves on the surface of the water. The waves spread outwards from where the stone hit the water.

Sounds also travel in waves. Sound waves are invisible. They push through the air, from the object making the sound, to your ears.

Work with a friend
Make a wave!

You will need:
2 long lengths of sticky tape
wooden lollipop sticks

Stretch a length of sticky tape – sticky side up – across a table top. Place lollipop sticks across the sticky surface. Now stretch another length of sticky tape – sticky side down – on top of the sticks.

Ask a friend to hold one end of the tape whilst you hold the other end. Tap one of the wooden sticks with a finger. Watch how the "wave" moves across to your friend.

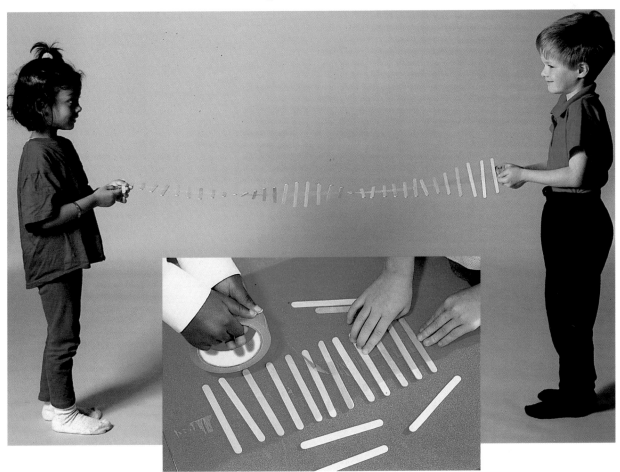

Can you hear it?

Look at the photograph. The teacher is striking a triangle. Which children can hear the sound of the triangle? Who can hear the loudest sound? Is the sound softer for some of the children? Are there some places where the sound could not be heard? Test your ideas.

Work with a friend
Now try this

You will need:
small radio
cardboard tubes
sticky tape

Turn the radio on so that it is playing quietly. Move away from the radio so that you cannot hear it play. Now walk towards the radio and stop when you can hear it. Mark this spot.

Now make a cardboard tube the same length as the distance from the radio to the spot you have marked. Listen to the radio through the long tube.

Can you hear the radio playing? Is it louder, softer or the same as it was before?

Why does this happen?

Hearing sounds

You hear sounds when they enter your ears. The part of your ear that you can see is called the outer ear. The shape of the outer ear enables it to collect sound waves. The sound waves then pass down a tube to delicate parts of your ear which are inside your head. Inside your ear the sound waves cause the eardrum to vibrate. From your eardrum sound messages are sent to your brain.

Work with a friend
Can you hear a pin drop?

You will need:
a pin or needle
a metal dish
a quiet room

Ask your friend to stand a long way behind you. Ask your friend to drop the pin on to the metal dish.

Did you hear the sound of the pin dropping? Let your friend move a pace towards you, and then drop the pin. Did you hear the sound?

Your friend should move forward, a pace at a time, until you can hear the pin drop.

How many paces between you and your friend?

Making sounds louder

These children are listening to music on a hi-fi system. They can turn a knob to make the music louder. The sound comes out through loudspeakers. Can you see the loudspeakers in this photograph?

Radios and televisions also have loudspeakers in them. When you listen to someone talking on the telephone you put your ear next to a loudspeaker.

Search for sounds

Cut out a square of card.
Roll the card to make a cone shape.
Use sticky tape to hold it in shape.
Cut a hole and insert the tubing. Make a
second cone and attach the tubing to it.

Hold one cone next to your ear and put the
other cone next to a ticking clock. Is the
ticking much louder now?

You will need:
thin card
scissors
plastic or rubber
 tubing
sticky tape
pencil

Find out more!
Listen to other quiet sounds
such as your heart beating,
someone whispering and
someone speaking on the
telephone. What other
quiet sounds can you
make louder?

Your voice

You can make lots of different sounds with your voice. Your voice comes from a part of the throat called the voice box or larynx. Inside the larynx are flaps called vocal cords. When you speak or sing your vocal cords vibrate. Your mouth and tongue help to make the sounds we hear.

Collect the sounds of human voices

Think of all the different kinds of sounds people can make. Here are some of them:

talking	singing
shouting	crying
sneezing	coughing
yawning	whispering

Can you think of more?
Use a tape-recorder to make a collection of these different human sounds.

You will need:
small tape-recorder

Find out more!
Make a tape collection of sounds made by different animals.

19

The sound of music

One way to make the sound of music is to sing. We also use musical instruments. These people are hitting their drums and making loud sounds. They hit their drums with sticks. The sticks make the skin of the drums, and the air inside, vibrate causing the sound. Can you think of other musical instruments that make sounds when they are hit, tapped or shaken? Make a display of some of these instruments.

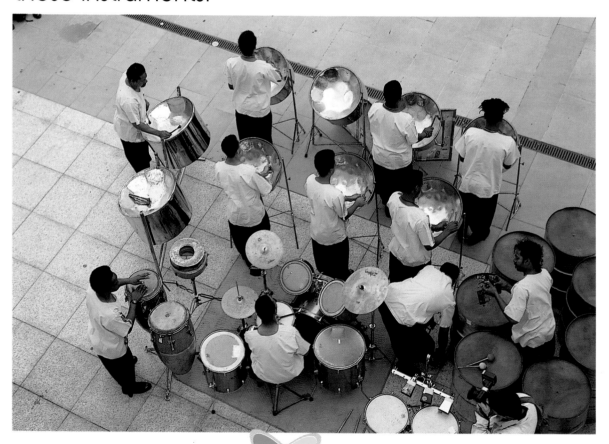

Make a plant-pot xylophone!

Hang the plant pots from the wooden pole.
Look at the photographs to help you.
Tap each pot with a pencil.
What differences do you notice in the sounds they make?
Can you tap out a tune ?
What happens if you hold a pot as you tap it?
Why does this happen?

You will need:
different-sized plant pots
string
nails
wooden pole
pencil

Blowing musical notes

You can make musical sounds by blowing. These children are blowing across the top of some bottles. Each bottle has a different amount of coloured water in it. When they blow across the top of a bottle it makes a musical note. Blowing across the top of the bottle makes the air inside the bottle vibrate. A long column of air vibrates to give a low note. Short columns give high notes. Collect photographs of musical instruments that work by blowing and making air vibrate.

Make a wind instrument

You will need:
short length of plastic tubing
cork
dowel rod or stiff wire

Push the wooden dowel rod into the cork.
Push the cork into the tubing. The cork needs to fit quite tightly into the tubing. Check that you can move it up and down with the dowel rod.
Now blow across the top of the tubing as you move the cork up and down.
What happens?
What is vibrating?
Why do the notes change?

Vibrating strings

Many musical instruments have strings stretched over a box or board. The strings are made to vibrate and make sounds. The sound box or sound board makes the sound louder. This guitarist is plucking the strings of her guitar to make sounds. Do any of your friends play string instruments? Ask them to show you how they make the strings vibrate.

Make a small guitar

You will need:
long cardboard
box with a lid
four elastic bands
eight brass
fasteners
scissors
pencil
small saucer

Place the saucer on the lid of the box and draw around it.

Ask an adult to help cut out a circular hole in the lid.

Push four brass fasteners into both ends of the box.

Fasten the elastic bands to the fasteners.

Make a cardboard "bridge" and push it under the elastic bands.

Pluck the bands. Listen to the sounds they make.

Stretch the bands tighter. What differences do you notice when you pluck the bands?

Sending sounds

You can send sounds to your friends by speaking softly or loudly. Sometimes you need to shout to send the sound further.

A telephone uses electricity to send sounds a long way. You can use a telephone to speak to a friend on the other side of the world!

Work with a friend
Make a simple telephone

You will need:
Two plastic cups
two paper clips
thin string
large pin

Ask an adult to make a hole in the bottom of each plastic cup, using the pin.

Thread the string through both holes. Tie a paperclip to each end so the string does not slip through the holes.

Whisper through one cup while a friend listens through the other cup.

Keep the string tight as you speak.

Can your friend hear what you are saying?

What happens if the string is loose?

How does your string telephone work?

Bouncing sounds

Sometimes when you shout in an empty room or in a subway you can hear your voice being repeated. This is the sound of your voice bouncing off the walls. It is called an echo. Find a place where you can make your voice echo.

Work with a friend
Make sound bounce

Ask your friend to hold the card upright.
Place the cardboard tubes at angles to
the stiff card.
Put a ticking clock near one of the tubes.
Listen at the end of the other tube.
Can you hear the clock ticking?
Sound, from the clock, travels down one
tube and bounces off the card into the
other tube. The ticking moves up this tube,
as sound waves, to your ear.

Index